Songs of Life and Living

Songs of Life and Living,
Poetic Reflections from the Spirit of a Man
Samuel Adewumi

Published by
Olushola Publishing

Cover, Design and Book Layout by Monica, Belle+Benton, Int'l
Cover Photo by Morenike Allen
Back Cover Photo by Olushola Adewumi
Bridal Photos compliments of
Nigerian Fabrics & Fashions, Brooklyn NY

Library of Congress Cataloging-in-Publication Data
Adewumi, Samuel A.,
  Songs of life & living : poetic reflections from the spirit of a man /
by Samuel A. Adewumi.
  p. cm.
  ISBN 978-0-9718191-8-4
  I. Title.
  PS3601.D48S66 2007
  811'.6--dc22
  2007017323

Olushola Publishing
P.O. Box 050238
Brooklyn, N.Y. 11205
website: www.songsoflifeandliving.com
Ph. (347) 789-4258

Acknowledgements

To my family, Auntie Liz, Bro Vic, Bro Joe, Sister Joyce, Eman, Bayo, Max, Bunmi, Isis, Junior and Rhema, thank-you for your support and understanding through all of this.
To my brothers in spirit, Sean, David, Horace, Kevin, Rodney, Brandon, Blayne, thanks for your openness, honesty and friendship through thick and thin.
Finally to my sisters, friends, loves, Yemisi, Tatia, Ngosi, Joanne, Pheta, Sharon, Kelly, Morenike, Julia, Monique and Kendra the experiences, knowledge and wisdom I have gained from you has been immeasureable and I humbly say thank-you. To my truly precious friend and talented editor and designer, Monica, you are a treasure. To my publisher, Guichard Cadet, thanks for walking me through this process, I am truly indebted to you. To all who have been a part of this process in so many different ways, I say thank-you and may the creator bless you as you have blessed me. Finally, to Dr. Ron Simmons, may your spirit rest in peace, and to Dr. James Turner, you both exemplified to a young anxious student what true black manhood represented: strength, intellect, determination, social consciousness and a deep unyielding love for our people.
I give thanks to the most high that I was touched by the light that shines so brightly from you both and pray that you and yours shall forever be blessed.

TABLE OF CONTENTS

Songs of Life and Living
"Poetic Reflections From the Spirit of a Man"

The worries of this world often cloud our ability to truly live and enjoy life. From the evening news and the daily newspapers to movies and videos we are currently reminded of the chaos, and seeming utter madness of the world we live in. For sure we are beset with societal, community and personal ills but we can never forget that there is still so much beauty around us. Whether it be in the faces or stories of the people we walk by every day, or the sight of a wondrous bed of flowers in an urban city block there is still so much for us to appreciate in this world that has been given to us, so much light still shines out for us to see, touch and taste. The most high has given us all a purpose here and part of our life's challenge is to discover and manifest that purpose for when we do, we bring forth another bright ray of light into this world, your world, my world, our world. I dedicate this book to that endeavor and pray that it brings both light and inspiration to your world.

Peace and Blessings

Samuel Adewumi

encounters

Two souls alight on the outstretched limbs
of the tree
a hint of recognition from a time long ago
was it a fleet encounter
or a lifelong embrace
was it as king and queen, friend of friends
or as wishful lovers bound by worldly
shackles
but chance or is it faith that brings them
together again on this tree
a gleam in each one's eyes
a longing of the ages
"perhaps"...one starts
but then the call is heard
the natural order of the universe
must be maintained
they alight with fluttering wings
for their journey is not yet complete
but before the wind carries them afar
he calls
my dear...I will meet you again.
Here in this space...in another time
here again...
On this tree of life.

PART ONE

Watching from across the floor
I stand, mesmerized by the beauty
My eyes behold
"By the gods!" I proclaim
Never have I seen such a woman
Beauty yes but even more so
The epitome of style, grace
And much that my mind is
Yet unable to fathom
On the dance floor she moves
Her full hips gently rolling
Creating their own sensual rhythm
Her supple shoulders roll too
Carefully supporting a most
Delicate and delectable neck
Ah and yes those legs
Gracefully weaving a sultry pattern on the floor
Entrancing me with their promise
Of the wonders they could lead me to
entrapping me within visions of soulful ecstasy
But to know her touch
To feel her warmth alongside my face
To taste the sweet nectar of her lips
To hold her close to my heart
And to love her oh so strong
This would fulfill my greatest desires in life
For I sense now how to become complete
I have found the other half of my soul
And now I must bring her home with me

It was...

Like I knew what she would say...
Like I knew what was in her mind...
Like I saw blue skies, white capped
mountains and rolling streams in her eyes.
Like I had butterflies in my stomach and
shivers on my shoulders.
Like she sang to me as she spoke,
a song of life, of living, of the joys and the
pains.
Like it was her life...like it was mine.
Like my words danced with her song
maybe the cha-cha, the boogie or even the
tango.
Like I knew her before, had shared many a
thought with
Like I just can't find the words to describe...
how good it felt
Like it was just a conversation
that lasted
like....five minutes.

What Would You Do?

What would you do
If we sat on the shore
Listening to the sea
Gently but persistently
Pounding the beach?

What would you do
If on a midsummer's night
We laid together under a
Moonlit sky gazing at the
Twinkle of the stars above?

What would you do
If during an autumn quell
We sat round the fireplace
While in the background
The steady rain tap, taps
On the windows
Reminding us of the wetness
Found outside?

What would you do?

I would
Desire you, need you, want you
Touch you, feel you, caress you
Kiss you, nibble you, taste you
And make love to you
For eternity on that day

Would you let me?

I Know...

I know I'm not supposed to
I know I should know better
I know I can do without
I know I should resist this temptation
I know all would ask why
I know they would disapprove
I know, I know, I know

I know how it would be
I know how it would start
I know hands would gently stroke
the other's face, neck, shoulders, arms, thighs
I know gentle kisses would shortly follow...
I know faces would touch cheek-to-cheek
I know lips would passionately open and
tongues explore each others warm depths
I know they would separate and leave to
explore backs, chest, navels and foreseeable treasures
I know bodies would embrace and open to each other
I know there'd be a bump, a grind, and yes, another bump
I know the moans would ring throughout, from deep, deep
inside, softly first but ever growing in intensity
I know there'd be a climax like waves ceaselessly cascading
into the shore
I know we'd lay in each other's arms, gently caressing and
sharing from within

I know I'd want to repeat this scene, over and over and over...
I know I'm not supposed to want this
I know I should know better than this...
But I don't..............

Silent Midnight

Silent midnight stars alight
Gentle wind caressing smooth ebony
Ibis feathers trail a path
Through fields of desire
Honey drips from its cone
Rich, succulent not a drop uncollected
Majestic portals open to receive
A strength born of divine will
Waves gently pounding the sea surf
The rhythm of raindrops
Stroking the outstretched lily
The oncoming storm churns the waters
Lightning sears through the midnight sky
The internal sacred fire rises to its pin-
nacle
Thunder releases its crescendo
Calling even the divine to testify
Silent midnight love aflight
Staring into my lovers starlit eyes

unsure...

Discovery, attraction, desire
the newness of it all
stronger than I could have imagined
thoughts spinning, futures conjured
mixing with my realities, matrixing my
space
Had wondered about her
if she desired me as I did her
but to myself my thoughts were kept
unsure if I would be ready for the answer

Her skin radiates with its own beauty
like honey on the tip of my tongue
my touch on her skin leaves me
flushed and full of desire
her touch the sweetest of sweet
sending waves through my being
Still wondering about her
If she desired me as I did her
but to myself my thoughts were kept
fantasies bound in pleasure and bliss

Yes, I do she said to me
Yes I do she quietly whispered again
I have dreamt of your touch
felt you hold me, kiss me, fill me
comfort to my spirit you are
companion to my soul in
its secret hiding place
But I wondered if you desired me as I did you
but to myself my thoughts were kept
unsure if I was ready for your answer

I would welcome your dive

wrapping you in my wings

shielding you, protecting you

while the essence of you

washed me pure

on an ivory cloud I would rest you

as sweet ballads flowed by

serenading us with tunes of hot summer

nights

and cool fall eves

with flashes of my desire

lighting up the twilight sky

feel you I would

caress you I would

stroke you I would

kiss you I would

love you I would!

Dream Lover

Bonfire of desire
Sweeping a path through my being
From whence it comes yet unknown
Searing through me
Leaving in its wake passion, want, need
Still yet its origin eludes me
A presence approaches
Soft and warm it gently reaches out
Kneading, caressing, touching
Releasing my needs, delivering my wants
And stroking my passion
Enveloping me within its folds
I succumb to its desires
An eternity passes as I move towards bliss
I begin to shudder as
Ethereal streams of energy pass through me
I am lifted as if by a wave
I rise higher, higher, ...
"Sweetie, Honey" I hear
"Sweetie" I hear again
My eyes gently open
There astride me, smiling down on me
Is my queen
Her eyes full of mischief
I realize all
Reaching for her
I bring her to me and
Again taste her lips,
The lips of my Dream-Lover

Sho Mo

{Sho mo ekan te mon sau}
Do you know what I mean
When I talk about this we, this us, this entity
that we created part of and yet separate
from you and I?

{She' un bough eekun ti mo wi}
Do you understand what I'm saying
when I say it needs to be fed and nurtured.
That it can't grow on its own...needing us as
parents to mold and shape its purpose and direction?

{Sho le' re' ikun ti mon re}
Can you see what I see?
The endless possibilities, the things "we" accomplish,
the joy we bring forth; joined together in mission
and purpose and blessed with the ability to manifest
our will as "we"

{Sh-ole shun to mi}
Can you feel what I feel?
when it comes under attack, by friends, family and even us
as it winces in pain under a steady assault of coldness, bit-
terness,
harshness, jealousy and even betrayal

{Shown mo ikun ti mon mo}
But even more, do you know what I know
That we are blessed for we will survive
That I can't and won't ever give "we" "us" up?
That through it all I stay committed and loyal to WE!
Forever in love with you, with me, with us!

This is a time of fast lives
With little meaning or purpose
Of shallow souls and hollow spirits
Where (wo)man's decency to (wo)man
Is tossed for the pleasure of self
Where the goal becomes more
Important than the journey
and the experience of life,
the joy of living,
is often taken for granted
where our intrinsic value can
only be measured by the physicals we
surround ourselves with
of plastic things, of plastic people
of motion without emotion
and friendships of years
wither but in days
This is a time of fast lives
with little meaning or purpose
of shallow souls and hollow spirits
a time of chaos and change
as wo(man) again falls from her (his)
heights
and the earth itself cries
and the earth itself cries!!

SIGNS OF THE TIMES

a fleeting thought
a fleeting thought
a fleeting thought
a fleeting thought

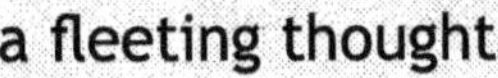

The fire of the dragon
is a magnet for those
whose minds are in
perpetual motion
it becomes such as the
food of the gods
for as they feast upon it
galaxies are formed
stars are affixed in the
infinite sky
and even worlds are
born and reborn

I say no more in this my reply
All else left for others to fathom
I think only of warm nights
Sunny breezes and gentle walks
Of overcoming and achieving
Of coming into myself, my true nature
Through the experience of your love
So I say no more in this my reply
For what more can be said?

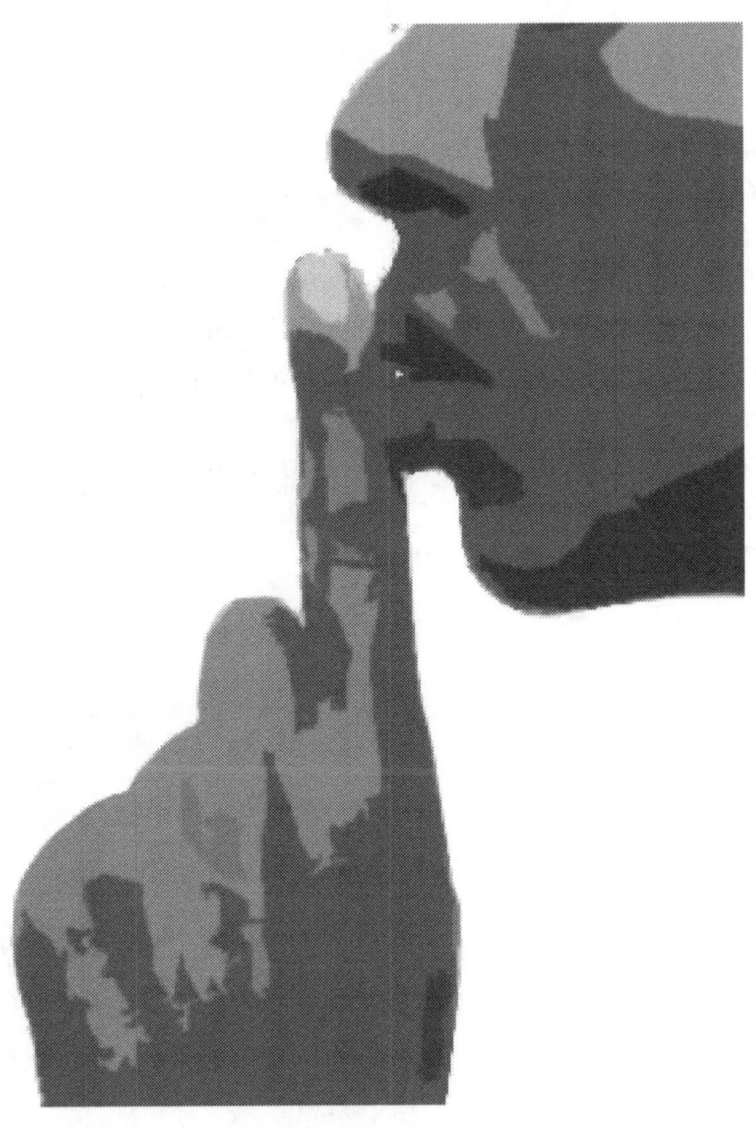

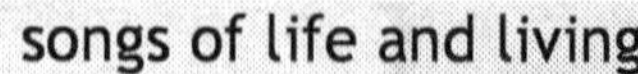

My darling, my heart
I wish to hold your sweet form
and taste the nectar of your lips
I wish to breathe from the same air you
draw
feel the wind that sweeps across your brows
and inhale the fragrance that is you
Oh for but that minute, that second to draw
near
when you again return to stroke my weary
head
and make me whole again.

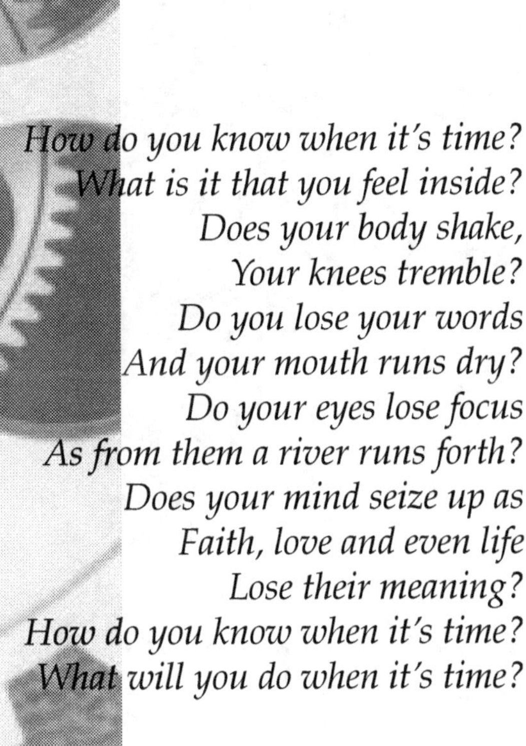

How do you know when it's time?
What is it that you feel inside?
Does your body shake,
Your knees tremble?
Do you lose your words
And your mouth runs dry?
Do your eyes lose focus
As from them a river runs forth?
Does your mind seize up as
Faith, love and even life
Lose their meaning?
How do you know when it's time?
What will you do when it's time?

Butterfly

Golden Butterfly
Cater What? Never!
Must Have
Just Become, Always Was
Forever Shall Be
My Golden Butterfly

THIS WONDROUS FLOWER
BLOSSOMS BEFORE MY VERY EYES
ENTHRALLED I STARE,
AFRAID EVEN TO SPEAK,
EVEN TO MOVE
LEST IT NOTICES MY FOCUSED
GAZE AND WITHDRAW
ITS WONDERS FROM ME
YET FROM A DISTANCE I STARE
LEST I EVEN SPOIL ITS GRACE
WITH A WORD, A MOVE, A PLAN
IN THE PRESENT I ADORE IT
IN THE PRESENT I DESIRE IT
IN THE PRESENT I CHERISH IT
IN THE PRESENT, IT IS MINE

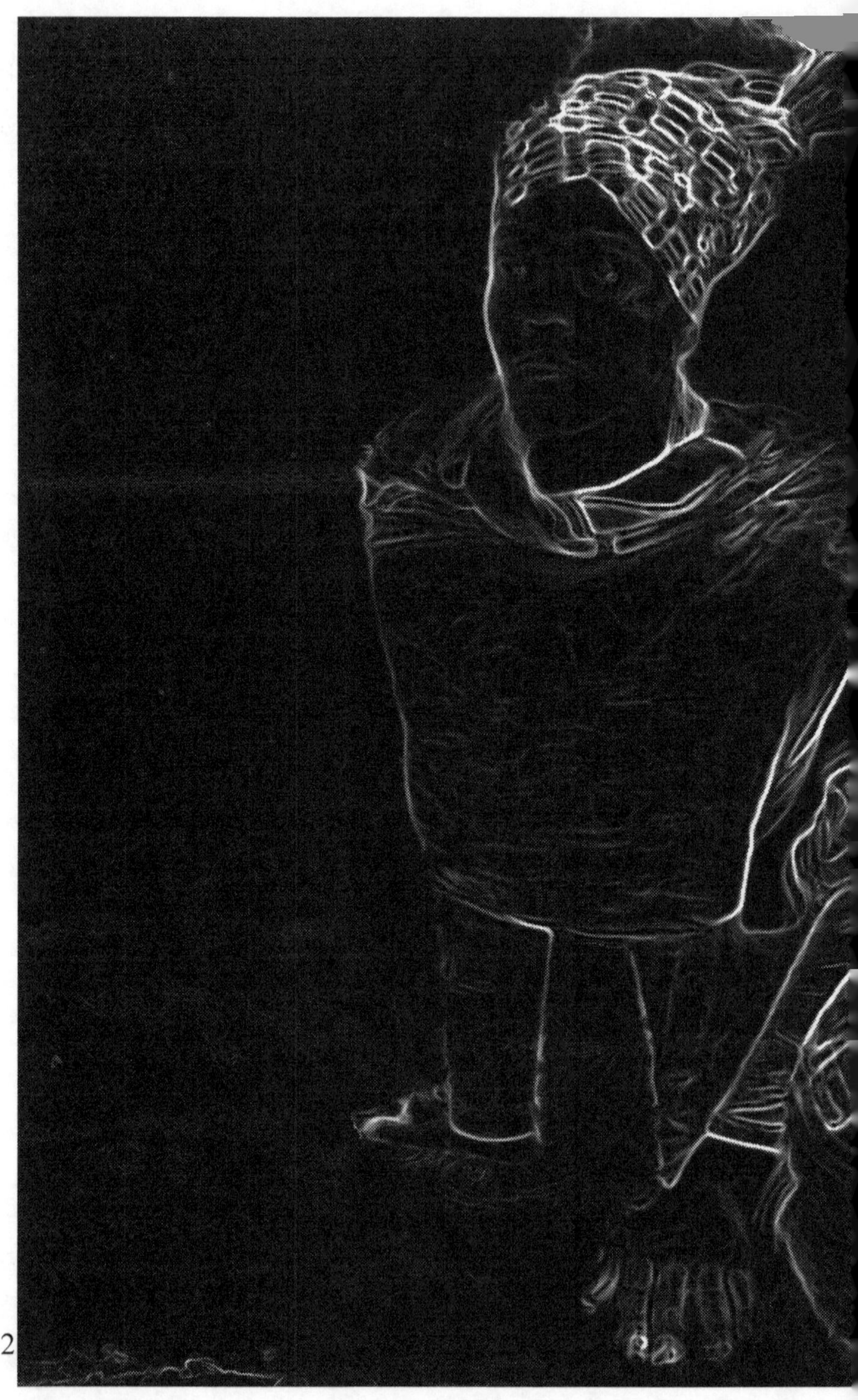

a quiet space

Princess of the Sea
Waves gently pound the sea surf
Advancing and retreating they perform
Their eternal dance with the sand
Their rhythm, both majestic and eternal
Calms my soul

Seagulls circle overhead
Suddenly they cry out and descend
Onto the beach
The receding water has again
Betrayed the lair of the sandcrabs
They scurry to redig new holes lest
They become the latest players in the
Circle of life

The evening sun dances on the waters
Reflecting a thousand shades of yellow, orange and red
Lighting up the skies with an aerial display
Full of billowing clouds
Masquerading as shape-changers

A presence shakes me from my meditation
Looking out I see her
Standing on a perch at the edge of the sea
A goddess in human form
True and indescribable in her beauty
She stood overlooking the waters
Head high and firm, hands at ample hips
Gracefully she raised her arms
As if to call to the sea itself
And indeed, it came to her
Gently lapping at her feet
Nimbly she climbed to a higher perch
Still the sea followed,
Gentle waves caressing her feet
Raising her hands again the sea began to retreat
A coy and knowing smile came to her lips
With the wind gently wrapping itself around her
She stood still, overlooking her domain
Daughter of Het-Heru, Beloved of Ntr
Princess of the Sea

Lessons

The love of experience
Is the love of life
To love life is to
Experience life

To experience life with you is to
Know fulfillment and completeness
The experience of life
Enriches and stimulates

The experience of you
Transforms my being
Uplifts me, causing me to
Rise higher and higher into
Consciousness of self and purpose

The only thing promised by life
Is the experience of life itself

The promise of you, together
Through this life, empowers
Invigorates and soothes me
And through all my experiences
Through my valleys, peaks,
Twists and turns
What I know, What I have come to realize
Is that my love of life is my love for YOU

L
isten

the language not yet formed
the sounds not yet heard
to describe the words of the heart
the heart does speak
but listen closely you must for
it speaks with the tongue of the soul
listen first you must
to the universal stillness
drown out all else and just.... listen
and surely as the sun does rise and command the
heavens each day
and the moon the earth each night
so shall you hear the voice of your own heart
so shall you hear the melody of your soul

Angel

Mighty trees reach up to the heavens
As the wind whistles through their leaves
While yet they wrest life from the sun
As they shield me underneath their breath

The light of the night sky fills up the void
I watch enthralled as the moon bathes me
With its translucent light while illuminating
The darkness that travels within the shadows

From the skies even the earth stands majestic
A patchwork of fields, valleys, waters, and
Canyons of awesome depths
And mountains of inspiring heights
Components of an awesome landscape
Testimony to the infinite from which it springs forth

As I marvel at that which has been placed here for us
As I wonder at the infinite beauty of this world
Even as I search this earth for the answers to questions
Many men dare not ask

I find myself most struck, most in awe, most in abject
wonder
By that which has manifested right before my eyes
For I never knew that angels still came to visit earth
Til the creator brought you into my life

Twinkle, twinkle little star
How I wonder who you are
full of wonder, joy and laughter
comedian, actress, star
wisdom beyond your years
and of course mouth too,
requesting, commanding, demanding,
assuming, consuming, acquiring
sometimes I wonder
"who's in charge here?"
Answering the business line,
"Can I help you?...hold on, or he's
not here right now".
Designing dress for you and mommy,
I'm looking forward to retiring quite early,
from the first word
to the first step and now
Nearing your fourth earth-day
I have seen you grow
Each day bringing more happiness and
Amazement with the things you say and do
and as I look at you now
quietly sleeping...
Still with a smile on your face
I thank the creator for my blessing,
for bringing me my own little STAR.

olushola

Of Ocean...

As the ocean washed my feet

With waves gently subsiding at the beach front

My thoughts of you as well

Cleansed me, opened me and moved me

Times like these give rise to introspection,

reflection

A wondering of what, how, why?

The ocean majestic in its vastness

With almost limitless capacity

Terrifying in onslaught and anger

Yet it too humbles itself

It too subsides and gives way

To another in its never ending dance

With its friend and foe ...

...and Sand

Humble and lowly in form
Has for centuries measured this ocean that
refuses to go away
Reeling from the steadfast push of
Waves it has stood its ground
refusing to be vanquished
Even at times befriending its mighty
assailant
Causing it to gently roll onto the beach
And wash over my feet
As the thoughts of my love
Still yet cleansed me, opened me and
moved me

For Ever
For Always
For Lovers...

Is it a feeling or an emotion
Grounded just in the mind or
Is there some biological manifestation
That gives credence to its reality?
The love of a brother
The love of a sister
The love of a child
The love of someone to whom you
Have pledged your heart
Even to pledge one's heart ..for the sake of love?
To reflect on a father's strong-handed love
Or a mother's warm, gentle love
Axioms like "love makes the world go round"
Even scripture vouches for it:
"For God so Loved the world"
Yet still the question,
What is love?
If I never find the answer to this question
Will I have lost out?
Will I have somehow been cheated of
That which must be so precious?
Or is it enough to know
That it is

For Ever
For Always
For Lovers

I find myself within myself
Only in those moments when I can brave
That which I know lies inside
I touch the center of my being
Only when my strength is available to me
Quiet moments gently expose that which I choose to
remain covered
In my solitude I find myself again
I see the reflection of my spirit on my heart
And feel a wrenching pain as it weeps within me

This life we live is uncharted
It provides no guarantees on what
We feel should be
We move based on faith,
On our supposed understanding
Even on the visages of wisdom, either ours or borrowed
But yet still we truly do not understand why
And cannot order our destinies
We move on though
And watch life unfold before us

In quiet reflection I again look inside
And see the loneliness within
There is an empty space, no a gaping hole
Where once something was, someone was
I feel the desire to fill that space again
But guard against this desire
To just fill it would take this precariously stable soul
Into a downward spiral as it
Consumes without discrimination
Looking to satisfy a hunger it does not fully understand
Trying to satisfy its thirst by gulping down rocks
Rather than that, assumed wisdom dictates
That the hole be carefully mended, be gently closed
And pray that the scars do not remain visible

Time is a gentle healer
It focuses, reshapes and comforts
It brings new understandings and realizations
Answers to questions that seemed unanswerable
Peace to a troubled spirit

I can now confront my pain
Assess and understand my loss
I release that which I have contained
And shed the tears that would not come
But I move close to my peace, my stability
Life has again done its thing
And I grow from this lesson
I decide I shall heal, and heal without scars
I choose to still love and be blessed through it

I keep a space open
Not a tattered gaping hole
But a smooth circular opening
A pathway that leads straight to the heart
Care resides within,
Love makes it its home
In there you shall remain
A permanent settler on the landscape of my spirit
And while yet I miss you,
Your presence, your energy, your spirit
I find my peace within this our resolvement
And move forward on this unpredictable
Often mad
Road called
LIFE

LOVE
HURTS

Irritation..

So there are a few things about me that "irritate" you?
I can work on them; now let's see what you can do for me
See though I may not always express it
And in case you didn't know
I suffer from this irritation discomfort as well
So just to put it on the table, let me share some thoughts with you
It irritates me when I call and you can't talk because you're
"busy" with a friend or "associate"
It irritates me that I usually get the professional and stoic voice
While your gentle and sweet voice is saved for others
It irritates me that when I needed you, you backed away from me
It irritates me that in times of crisis you still isolate yourself
Though I have always tried to be by your side
It irritates me that I also have my share of problems and burdens
But you will hardly ever feel the effect of them
It irritates me that I don't get as much
Affection from you as I need
That you don't touch me, hold me, like I need you to
It irritates me that with all the love I've tried to give and show
you it may not be enough
It irritates me that I'm not sure right now where we are heading
It irritates me that I don't know if this is
Just another hurdle or has our fuse run out?

And finally...it irritates me that I even feel the need to write this
Because all I want to do is keep on loving you.

Alone

Honey-covered raindrops
here used to fall,
hear now
silent footsteps
in the shrieking wind,
barren land, devoid of fruit
nectar dried,
sand, dust, ashes
the last survivors of yesterdays.
Celestial beams hidden by somber mists,
joy, happiness?
What manner of strange beasts are they?
Not so long ago
we were
here, there, now, then.
But now I am,
alone!
My heart be still,
My soul empty,
I shall forever
Miss You

Ahh, it hurts

This feeling in my pits,
Wrenching my insides.
Dammmm, it hurts
This pain in my chest, squeezing my heart,
My breath short and hurried
My face flushed and heated.
Why this feeling rendering and ripping
My soul, my spirit
Yes my soul wounded and bruised returns to
me
Its play is over, its mate is gone
I question now the wisdom of the ancients
When they said, "It is better to have loved
and lost
Than to have never loved at all"
No, they must not have known the love I
knew,
One that carried away my own spirit into
Joyful bliss and unearthly passion,
One that shook my core with its power and
strength
Yes, one that connected us through time and
space
No, they never knew this, never felt this
For its loss transcends the physical, even
the mental
It scatters my spirit through the ethers
I lay broken and shattered, without will to
move on
With hope only in the will of my creator
Ahhh, it hurts…

Damn! It hurts…

Lament to Ntr

Ntr, See my tears hear my cries
For the pain and suffering I have caused
For the blood oozing from my welts
as whips of anger and torment crisscross about my back

Ntr, See my tears hear my cries
For the past filled with so much anticipation
For the present that is no more
For the future, aborted in its first trimester of existence
It had no chance, as the bloodied blade of fate ripped
through its being
dissipating the souls united in convoluted embraces of
pleasure and bliss

Ntr, See my tears, hear my cries
I weep for the love I once knew
I cry for love I will know no more
Deliver me from my misery
Deaden this bleeding heart if you must
For the burden of its pain doth take over all other senses
I have eyes but I can not see
I have ears but I cannot hear
I have lips but I cannot taste
My nostrils have lost all scent
My skin has lost all sense of touch
I walk as one not of the living

Ntr See my tears, hear my cries
Heal your son, forsaken and alone
Grant me victory over the demons of despair that give chase
Give me strength to one day live again
Give me courage to one day love again

love hurts

I'm hurting from a place deep inside
So deep I didn't know it existed
Wasn't even sure what itwas when it started
Just had all these thoughts
All these words I need to express
All these things I wanted to talk about
Wanted to talk about love
What it means to me, how deep and personal
it is for me to say "I Love You"
How my love is unfettered and steadfast
Needing nothing else but your love in return
Wanted to talk about relationships
About how beautiful they can start
Almost magical and unreal in their purity
How they too often turn into
Stress-filled emotional roller coaster rides
Forcing early, unpredictable bail outs and abandonments
Wanted to talk about respect and caring
So crucial in any relationship
How it's vital that they be maintained
For disrespect and an uncaring heart
Undoubtedly tear down the very fiber
Of any relationship
Wanted to talk about you
How high I fly when we are in harmony
How low I can get when we are in discord
Wanted to talk about our future
Wondering if maybe we are trying too hard
That maybe it's just not meant to be for us
Wanted to talk about struggle
About whether or not what we have
Is worth fighting for
Realizing that love is work
But like a well-tilled and watered field
It produces such plentiful crops and wondrous realities
These burdens weigh heavily on my spirit
as I search now for you
I just want to sit with you
Just want to gaze into your eyes
Just want to reach out and touch you
Just want to talk
Just need to talk...

My Lord, My God, why hast though forsaken
me
A promise was made to me
This road I would never again tread
I've been here for more than my share
For sure I have carried the burden, perhaps even
the curse
Of those I have yet to know and of those I will
never know.
I have been trampled upon and yet I have arisen
I have been spat upon and yet I hold my head high
I have been cast aside while gold does yet shimmer
on my skin
This suffering was to be no more
This anguish to never fill this heart again
She was all I ever sought
A gift from the creator, of beauty, of grace, of
intellect
The answer to my prayers
The deliverance I so longed for
The joy no longer denied
Cherish her I did, like none before her
My soul was hers to take
My heart for her it pumped
My love for her was unbounded

i am available

love hurts

My life to her I gave freely
No woman have I ever loved so strong
No woman ever will I love so hard
But my life, my love, my heart, my soul
Have been returned to me
"I need these not, I want these not",
The words that echo through my mind
Drumming an incessant rhythm
That threatens my sanity
I desire this pain no more
I wish no more this suffering
New tears join old tears down
The inlets of this weary visage
In spontaneous discharges of grief and sorrow
I wish to no longer make forays into this battlefield
Misfortune forever has tamed my desire
I strike that word from my personal dictionary
Love for this soul carries a price
It can no longer afford to pay
Let it be for those whose hearts are still light and wistful
Let it be for the young, the hopeful, the fervent, the passionate
Let it be for those untainted dreamers who have yet to feel its
torrid bite
This heart though has bled its last drop
This soul has flown its last flight
The store chest is finally emptied
Forsake me not oh lord in my time of need
Your child, your son calls out for you
Set my feet, guide my footsteps
Free me from this seeming bondage
And heal this grieving heart

I am available to you
I am available to you

Silent Tears

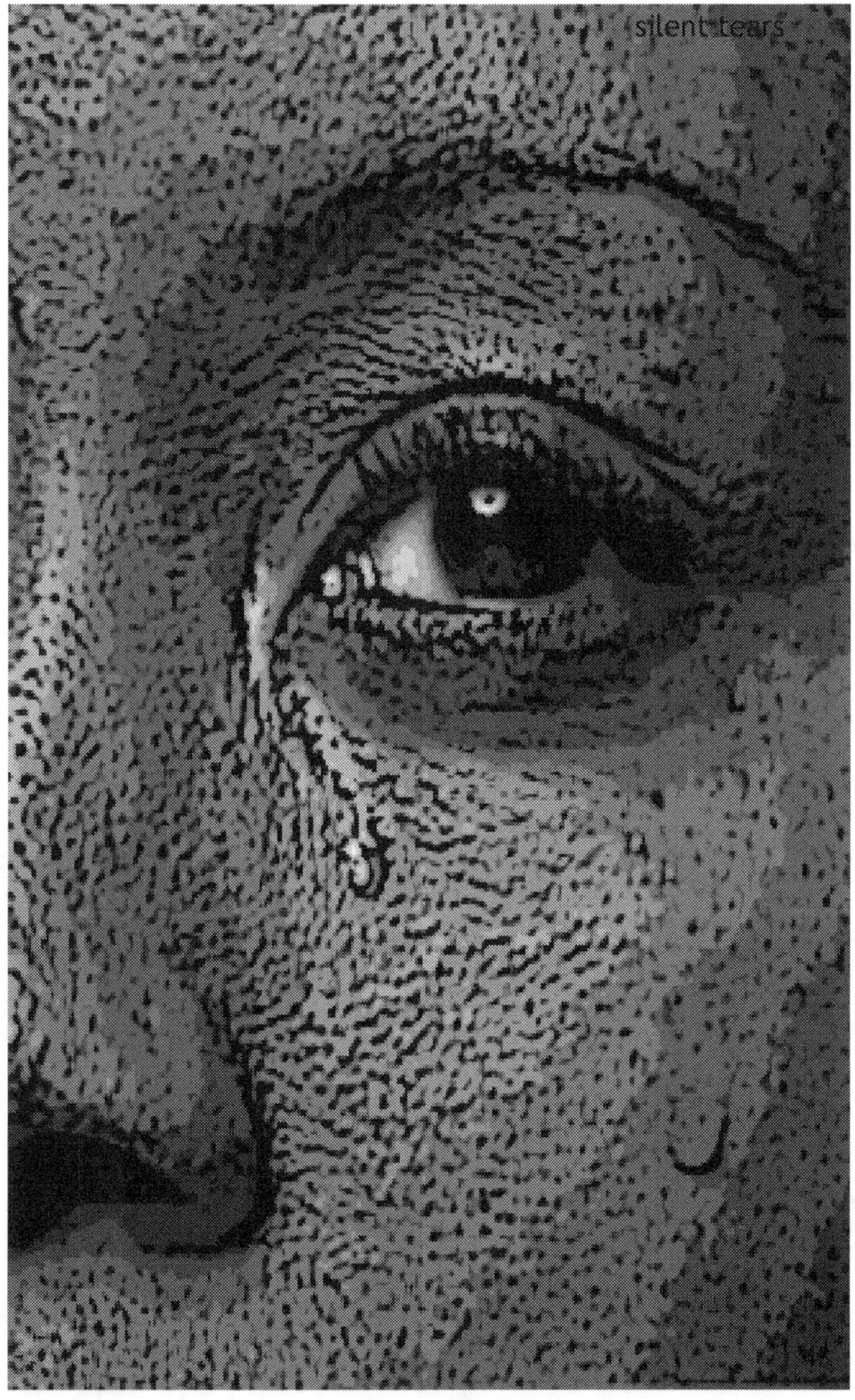
silent tears

It's Time

My people cry out in torment
Feel the sting of prickled thorns
Pressed round their brow
Anchored round their weary feet
The remnants of a strange and cruel bondage
That stained their minds
Corrupted their souls
And shackled their dreams
It's time

My people turn against themselves
Self-hate is reared in the bosom of mothers
Who know not what it is to love
Or be loved
Self-hate is seeded in the groin of fathers
Who have never been tended and
Know not how to tend
The salvos launched against each other would bring
Down the great wall itself
In this battle without victory
Just anguish, hurt, death and shame
The offspring of
Deceit, deception and game
It's time

My children cry out
Born to a world unwanted
Suckled onto a world of madness
The hope of tomorrow
Locked in the misery of today
The joy of youth, freedom, discovery
To dance on the rays of sunset
Or whisper to the stars themselves
All have been forgotten, stolen destroyed
Left only with steel gray images
Plastic flowers and canvas streams
They sleep but do not dream
They live but are without life
It's time

I wish to cry no more for my people
I wish to no more live with sorrow
I wish for this pain that wretches my heart to be gone!
I wish for my joy derailed, to arrive

It's time, it's time

Rise up oh ye once mighty and noble people
Wake from your slumber, the time has drawn nigh
The hour of our redemption is at hand
Rise from your sleep oh great king and queen
Come to arms my generals, gather your warriors
Summon them and make them ready
Gather your tools oh great surgeons
The wounds are many on the souls of my people
For centuries they have bled from within their spirit
With speed hasten now oh healers
The time for healing has arrived
The trumpet has been sounded
Our atonement has been received
Our deliverance is upon us

The Lord has spoken
Power has been returned unto us
Courage is again ours
Knowledge and wisdom have found their way home again
Our souls will heal
Our spirits will heal
Our bodies will heal
Mothers suckle your children on the
Milk of abundance and plenty
Fathers sire your children with the
Spirit of hope and love
Our families shall rise up,
United from within, united for without
Like the mighty crest leading the ocean wave
We shall break the world from its madness
And free tomorrow from its dreary cage
Our children will learn how to breathe again,
Our children will learn how to dream again,
Our children will learn how to live again

It's time,
It's our time

In the moment
the song of birds perched high
among the rain forest
does contend with the
chatter of monkey clans just below

In the moment
weary travelers stop the caravan as the long sought
after oasis is discovered deep within the Sahara
as the moon discloses the sand dunes
yet to come

In the moment
another blast is heard and the ground itself shakes
as the might of missiles
intended but for a few hiding in caves
destroys what took the earth
hundreds of years to build
in but the blink of an eye

In the moment
a hungry child cries aloud
another anguished mother wails
and a broken father weeps within his misery
unable to provide even a morsel
in a world yet full of Bush's and Hilton's
and Rockefeller's and Jordan's, and..., and..., and....

In the same moment
a seeker sits cross-legged in a secure space
having been full, having been empty
now in search of "I am"
In I am there is absolute peace,
absolute love, absolute consciousness
with the soul connected back to its source
I am becomes one with creation
unbounded, unfettered, infinite
with the mind paused, the ego fades and the seeker
lets go..lets go....

In this moment
birds sing while monkeys chatter
thirsty men stop to rest and drink
landscapes are changed by conflict
hungry children cry while mothers weep
a seeker has found their way
has experienced "the moment"
and the thread of destiny
brings another closer to home
...In this moment

WHO SHALL SPEAK?

Oh what a mighty people!
What a miracle of God you are,
That he himself must often
Stop and marvel at his work

People of beauty and sweetness of form
Complete with all the hues of the darkened rainbow
The prototype from which all others
Were duplicated but never replicated

People of knowledge, wisdom and understanding
The forefathers and foremothers of civilization
From whose loins sprung forth
Science, mathematics, medicine, philosophy and spirituality

People of compassion and consciousness
You opened your doors to those in need,
To the weary traveler, to the lost and forborne
Even yet as they conspired to violently seize
What you had so freely given

People of ingenuity and foresight
You chartered the course of the stars
And used it to navigate the great oceans
Spreading your culture and knowledge to
Your long removed sons and daughters

People of strength and fortitude
Who withstood the greatest atrocity
Man has ever committed against man
Kidnapped and stolen from your birthplace
You survived a treacherous inhumane passage though
You saw thousands if not millions of
Your people perish in the waters
You endured through chattel slavery
The most repressive and unjust form of slavery
The world has ever known
You where beaten, bloodied and abused
Your women raped, your men whipped and hung
You fought in wars, securing freedom
While still yet had not your own

48

Great people who else but you
Would be this testament to the power of the most high
For the creator has seen fit to lay his hand upon
You and declare to the world
" Try what you may to these my Chosen People,
Yes, you have raped, plundered and killed, but surely as
I am the Lord God, My people will rise, their spirits
Will never be vanquished, their souls will never be crushed

Oh you people,
You descendants and offspring of mother Africa
You have come through trials and tribulations
Too numerous to name
The souls of your fathers, your mothers
Your sons and daughters taken before their time, they cry out
They cry out for justice, they cry out for restitution
They cry out for remembrance,
They cry out for the future of their people
Who amongst you will hear their cry?
Who amongst you will give voice to their lamentations?
Who among you will speak for them?

"WE SHALL SPEAK!" answer the men of these people
Speak now then oh men
Make a joyful sound unto the Lord and
Deafen those who would
Still look to oppress and violate you
Speak now, like you've never spoken before
Speak with the voice of Fredrick Douglass,
Of Booker T. Washington, of Marcus Garvey , of
Malcolm X and of Martin Luther King
Speak with the voice of your great orators, your teachers, your ministers
and bring truth and liberation to your people
Speak now with the voice of the fathers who
Struggle to provide for and lead their families
Speak for your brothers who live their lives
In penitentiaries, for them emancipation was a cruel joke
Slavery is alive and well, even today

Who else shall speak?
"We shall speak!" cry out the women of these people
"We shall shout to the heavens themselves
For we have made a covenant with the Lord our God
And we shall not be forsaken, no never again"
Speak then oh mothers of God's people
For you carry the tale of your history in your wombs
It is you that passes the DNA of greatness to all you birth
Speak with the voice of Harriet Tubman, of Sojourner Truth,
Of Phyllis Wheatley, of Fannie Lou Hamer
Speak now oh daughters of women forced to raise and nurture
The offspring of others, while theirs were stolen away and sold
Speak mothers who do battle every day for the souls, spirits and
Lives of your children against a world
That seeks to denigrate and steal their humanity

And so the chosen people of God spoke
Ohh what a mighty sound it was
For they spoke the way only they can
And they sang the way only they can
And they danced the way only they can
And they played those drums the way only they can
And those from far and wide stopped and listened
God himself heard and began to weep for his people
Showering the gathering with his tears
Till one mighty among them beseeched him to stop
Lest he disperse them before the last speaker spoke

And so the last speaker moved towards the people
A child she was, yes just a child, but she spoke such
"My fathers, my mothers, my brothers, my sisters
Thank-you for all you have done for us
Thank-you for your blood, your sweat, and your tears
Thank-you for your unconquerable spirit, and your head yet unbowed
Your courage, fortitude and dignity has been our lantern
Your intellect, creativity and skill our torch
Your prayers our beacon of hope
We shall never forget the richness of our heritage
Nor the beauty of our legacy
Long shall they write about this our people
Many the songs to celebrate our story
But a new day has arisen
And this dawn brings renewed faith
We the children will join you in this struggle
We shall arm ourselves with the sword of the spirit
And defend ourselves with the shield of faith
We shall invoke that holy covenant and
Call the most high to our side
Our victory is sealed, our destiny revealed
Never again to be downtrodden
Never again to be scorned
Never Again!

Light the Fire! Onward we march! Light the Fire!

Us Black Folk

What has this world come to?
Drug dealers, crack heads, dope fiends
Transmitting STD's to children
Homeless men on the street
Talking bout how their baby momma's left them
And then put them in jail for fifteen years
What happened to the words of
Malcolm X, Martin Luther King Jr.
And Marcus Mosiah Garvey?
The ones that told us to stay strong
And be proud of who we are
The ones that made this America realize
That we are all created equally
They made it possible for us to have rights
And live freely
What...Happened...To dem words?
Look at us black folks
Killing our brothas
And molesting our sistas
Let's take a step back and realize
What we've done
What they've done
Remember Emmett Till?
The black boy who was beaten, shot and hung
Cause he supposedly whistled at a "white" woman
Yet those black men still go 'round
Drooling over dem women
Don't we remember our past?
Don't we think bout our future?
What's up with us black folk
What is happenin'?

by Olushola Adewumi

52

silent tears

We suffer quietly in our anguish
Our voices muffled by the pain
That crashes through our bodies
Under the whips, the clubs the instruments
They torture and torment us with

We suffer loudly in our anguish
Hear the screams of the men
Hear the yells of our children
As night raiders swoop down upon us
And the women mourn
For loved ones they shall never lay eyes upon
In this existence

Our spirits they seek
So for this they humiliate us, degrade us
Torture us
To steal our souls their goal
To take our humanity, our good
Our passion , yes even our lives

But they know us not, these invaders from the north
In our waters , two mighty oceans come and meet
As they acknowledge each others greatness while
Yet jostling for position
Each refusing to give up one inch of ground
Do they not know that we are their children?

But they know us not, these boars from distant lands
Children of the earth
We tamed the rivers, the lands
Even the mighty lion gives way in our path
We ruled this land justly before they arrived
And rule it again we shall even before they leave

Listen closely and hear the songs of Soweto,
Of Johannesburg, of Capetown
Look closely into the eyes of the mothers,
the Fathers the children
Look for their spirits, look for their souls
See them alive, radiant and powerful

They were wrong, oh so wrong
It was not theirs to take
These spirits that give us life
That gave us the courage to persevere
In the face of atrocity after atrocity

It was not theirs to take
These bodies of earthly form
Fashioned in the smiths of life's creation
Strong, resilient, powerful
Bend us yes, break us never!

We will rebuild this our world
Laid under siege for far too long
We are the people of this land,
We breath its air, till its fields and
Return to it when we are called home
We shall rise, yes we shall rise

Hear now the cries of my people
From village to village
From shore to shore
From the mountains to the fields
Hear their cries now
Of freedom, of hope, of faith
Viva Africa!!, Viva Azania!!

songs of life
songs of life
songs of life
songs of life
songs of life

IN OUR HEARTS

This poem
First thanks Mutabaruka
For the first This Poem
This poem woke me up
Early one morning to
Write this poem
This poem is about life, about living
About loving, about joy
This poem is not sad, not angry
Not regretful, not hateful
This poem says thank-you
To all who have had a hand in
Writing this poem
This poem is vibrant, is alive
It comes from itself and knows no end
This poem rolls like thunder
And flashes like lightning
This poem celebrates something new,
Something old,
What was here all along but just now discovered
This poem needs to speak!
This poem brought you to me
Those many years ago
When I did not know you
So close but yet so far
Separated by fields worn under by
Rambling feet passing over
This poem kept you a secret from me
It told me you were there
But not where to find you
Not yet, not till now
This poem taught me well
For all my experience was in preparation
For what this poem knew all along
This poem taught me passion, conviction
How to invest with mind body and soul
This poem taught me how to speak
To open my heart, open my mind
To be unafraid and willing
This poem taught me of reflection
Of introspection, of meditation
To change for the sake of
Being that much closer to
That which I was born to be
This poem taught me of need
Of fire and desire
It opened up this heart and led it to
Joy and pain
And played in my mind with thoughts
Of a love, forever for always

This poem led me to that which is spirit
Within and without,
To the infinite connection that is
The Most High
This poem is of the past and that which I
Have learned
This poem is of the present and that which I do
This poem is of the future and that which I hope and pray for
This poem is about what you will say to me in 6 months,
in 6 years, in 6 decades and in 6 lifetimes
This poem is about how much more
You become a part of me in one week and
How much more you will be a part of me
Every one week for evermore
This poem is about My completeness
When You lay in my arms
This poem is about my content when I
Touch you
This poem is about my peace
When you touch me
This poem is about my passion for you
So different this time
It rumbles in its quietness
Yet unyielding in its presence
It wants all of you, now, today, right here, right now
But it is patient for it knows this is not just about today,
this is about tomorrow
And all the tomorrows after that one
And this time.... we get it right
This poem says that I am committed to
This our process, of discovery
Of realization, of wonder
This poem says I never want it to end
This poem says that I want every week to be
My first week with you
Every smile, our first smile
Every touch, our first touch
Every kiss, our first kiss
This poem says that you are the Queen
That was fitted for my Crown
This poem ask that you take your space in
My Kingdom
This poem will sing our song
from here and will continue on
even past these words
for this poem will continue
In...Our...Hearts

COMMITMENT

Sometimes I wonder
why I go through this
why I have taken this path
on the road of what some may call love.
Its a hard road, full of twists and turns
and gut wrenching ups and downs.
Look closely on this road lest
you be pricked by that so seemingly
beautiful rose.

Listen closely while you travel for the mouth
that often brings you so much pleasure can
crush your spirit but with a word...
but despite this and other yet unspeakable
sometimes unfathomable perils,
on this road I tread.

Its the promise this road makes
that keeps me going forward;
its a promise that along this road
I will find comfort, appreciation, respect,
care, compassion, need, release and a host of
feelings, emotions and experiences too
extensive to completely list

This promise is sealed with but
one thing...commitment!
without it the journey on
the road ceases...
So as I come to you now
my heart bare, exposed, overflowing with
love for you as does the river overflows onto its bank
I stand committed to our journey, our road, our love.
I have but one question, *"Are you committed?"*

MIDNIGHT BLUE

In you, in me without border, without skin
Feel you, feel me, like a synchronized rhythm
Without beginning, without end, just is, just being
A complex arrangement of translucent energy
Vibrating with all the hues of midnight blue
Engaged in the dance of omnipresent reality
Hear the roar of the waterfall mimic the beat of the heart
Feel the gentleness of touch as Ibis plumes
Flutter in the breeze coming forth from the flowing rivers
Against the backdrop of destiny and purpose
Emotion raises forth its regal head
Devotion lays claim to all it sees
And Love rules, Manifest and Absolute !!

I find you

I find you filled with perspective,
Directness and wisdom
I find you filled with gentleness and kindness
I find you filled with humor and laughter
I find you able to teach with a smile
To offer differing views with candor
Yet with a simplicity that builds not break down
I find in your voice sultriness and seduction
Powers that render me harmless
I find in your actions the promise of
Warm touches and gentle hugs
I find you completely filling and delicious
And desire for this poem not to end

Still There?

As I laid there gazing at
the beauty that was you
thanking my creator for sending such as you to me
I began to reflect on all that
you bring to me
all that you do and have done and will do
and realized that yes indeed you where for me
but my doubts arose
was I the one for you?
and in the formation of the thought
the answer itself was given
that for me to bring to you the joy
you have brought to me
I must uplift my spirit and harmonize my soul
allow it to glide as the winged eagle does glide
soar to the sun itself on but a whisper of air
unbound and unfettered is how i need to experience you
that the love that flows out so easily from you
may meet the torrent of love that gushes from my essence
and so my divine mate
having worked and toiled
having lived and learned
and after much joy and pain
I find myself finally ready to receive you and to give me
are you still there?
are we still there?

question not...

You would question my miss of you
Question next my love of you?
Know you not the source and measure of
this love?
From the ancient banks of the
Tigris-Euphrates
Came the waters of this
current that flows through my heart
From the never-ending sands that receive
the inundation of the Blue and White Nile
Does it owe its magnitude
To the majesty of the cliffs and snow
capped peaks of   Mount Kilimanjaro
Does it owe its breadth
Question first if snow will come in
January
Question next if roses will bloom in May
But to you, my scarab
The divine olive tree that grows in my
garden of Treasures
Question not my love of you

Alas, question not my miss of you!!

ONCE AGAIN

INTO THIS SPACE I ENTER
FILLED WITH ANTICIPATION, WONDER AND DESIRE
STRENGTH AND WILL ARE REQUIRED
FOR IN THIS SPACE THE UNKNOWN RESIDES
ENDLESS POSSIBILITIES HARNESSED AROUND HARSH
REALITIES
NEED ARISES TO STAY YET UNFULFILLED
THE HEART BEATS WILD WITH LONGING
FOR THE GENTLE STROKE YET TO BE FELT
QUESTION WHY DO I ENTER
WHY NOT INTO A SAFE SPACE
WHERE THE ROAD IS WELL PAVED
DIRECT AND STRAIGHT
BUT WITHOUT PASSION, WITHOUT DESIRE
THAT WHICH YOUR SPACE BRINGS ME
IS THE FIRE THAT LIGHTS THE NIGHT SKY
THE WIND THAT COOLS THE SWELTERING AIR
THE BALM THAT QUIETS THE ANGRY STORM
COMPANION TO MY SPIRIT
I FEEL YOU WITHOUT TOUCH
I SEE YOU WITHOUT EYES
I KNOW YOU WITHOUT WORDS
NOT MUCH CAN I ASK FOR
THOUGH MUCH MORE I CAN GIVE
THE MOMENTS I DO RECEIVE I TREASURE
FOR IN THAT SPACE, IN THAT TIME
ONCE AGAIN YOU ARE MINE

TRAVELLER

I wish to not embark on this journey
That will take me away from my heart
I desire to remain but here
Inhaling the sweet fragrance of your being
But duty does overwhelm my desire
And go I must

I longed for you even as I released you from that last embrace
Still yet feeling the pulse of your heart
Beating besides mine
The moon will spend many a night with you,
Raindrops will splatter and cascade at your feet
The songs of birds announcing the coming of
The morning sun will rise you from your slumber
And even the seasons will pass through your fingertips
Many times before I feel that oh so sweet beat again

The miles between us increase each passing minute
I reach out my hand for you but
I know not where you are
I have yet to accept this loneliness
My heart fathoms not that you are not here
It cries out for you and waits for your answer
And waits, waits, ...waits
I count the days backwards to my return
Knowing not from where to start
My nights are spent in dreams
I wish not to wake from
Like the butterfly flirting with its flower
You dance across the landscapes of my consciousness
Forever in youth, beauty and grace

In two worlds I find myself
The one of my fate and destiny
Of the duty that still yet calls me
Having multiplied our space and time
By a matrix of the nth degree

In the other, I lay with you
Our limbs and bodies intertwined in loving embrace
I yet feel the taste of your lips on mine
Yet still shudder as you trace
Pathways through my being
In that world my heart never leaves yours
My spirit is unfettered and unbounded yet
It too is filled by the life you pour into it

The duality of my existence
Being and non being, love and duty
Self and selflessness
Like the primordial beat
That gives rise to the fundamental rhythm
Which harmonizes life itself
Two worlds locked into one existence
The dormant volcano ready to erupt unless
these whirlwind forces and emotions be resolved

And in the second, of the minute, of the hour in that day
That which has called me has at last being met
I stand triumphantly on fate but for a moment
Lest I tarry on my way home
Make haste! make haste! I cry
On the back of the wind yet I fly
Defying earth , ocean and sky
Onward I press, each passing second
Shall bring me closer to that which my spirit
Has yearned for

At last in my arms again I find you
Small rivers form through my closed eyelids
As I again feel your heart beat into mine
I drink from the wine guarded by your lips
And become as one intoxicated by its sweetness

Each Time

Each time I speak your name
Each time I see your face
Each time I hear your voice
Each time I catch your scent
Each time I kiss your lips
Each time I think of you
The taste of sweet nectar runs true in my mouth
Visions of sultry moonlit nights fill my eyes
A melody so sweet and pure runs true in my ears
The stimulating sweet aphrodisiac fills my nostrils
The weight of soaring clouds falls true on my lips
An eternity of bliss fills my mind
Each time I am with you
I know where heaven is!

Ode to my love

darling
You are precious
a gem of a woman
You have been hidden for too long
I marvel at what your transformation will uncover
and I desire to be there with you
for as you transform
so too will I
Reflection of my higher self you are
Complement to my needs
In you I discover
my wishes, my desires
my balance, my truth
Let all that is good thrive between us
and let all others pass away
And as the winds of time
have no end and know no beginning
Let what we now share
be of the same measure
I welcome this our circle
I welcome this our love

My eyes have been dreaming,
For so long they have
In them behold an image of sheer splendor and form
Created by years of longing, months of need, weeks of prayer
Days of fasting and seconds of deliverance
An image of such beauty have they created
They dare not awake, and I stay ever-yet
Dreaming

My mind has been wrapped,
For so long it has,
Contained in a virtual vortex of anticipation and anxiety
Questions play a continuous symphony on the strings of quiet thought
How?, when?, where? the desire to know ,
To find that which to now has been so elusive
To introspect the reasons and come to over-standing
Wrapped, as if in a cocoon
It is bounded and restrained but yet
Internal transformations occur in spontaneous combustions
Steadfastly advancing this mind to the time when it shall be
Unwrapped

My heart has been longing,
For so long it has
It has been wounded by the empty trails left by discarded journeys
Forays into a wilderness of thoughts and emotions
Without resolution or fulfillment
An abyss occupying the center of this heart
It cries out "No More, No More!!"
It aches for the peace it so desires
And seeks to lay claim to the love it longs…. the love it longs

Man knows not the times of his destiny
Knows not the hours of his fate
If counted one second differs not from the next
But when realized each second brings with it
New breath, new thought, new life
Each one vividly unique from the one before it and the
The one still yet to come

I knew not when I would see you
But see you I knew I would
Beheld you I did, in those eyes that refused to open
Closed in a dream of bliss and joy
Afraid to separate those eyelids lest you disappear
Now I need that dream no more

For the reality of your existence
Is now manifest
But dream on I shall
Of the times yet to be had with you
Of the wonder I will behold as my soul
Dances yet another dance with yours
Dreaming....

Unwrapped now from its cocoon
The wings of a monarch begin to beat
Reborn with the knowledge of its purpose
It lifts itself effortlessly and
Moves forward, advancing ever yet to its destiny
So does the unfettered, unwrapped mind
Advance forward, the questions answered, the way known

Long no more oh valiant heart
Heal thy wounds and lock the
Doors to those aimless paths
Lay down your burden and cry no more
Rather beat anew with the thirst for life and the sense of purpose
Thy peace , so long sought for, has been delivered
Join now with the heart of your destiny , your true path awaits

Behold the golden door that appears
Before hidden by somber clouds and swirling mists of mystery
It's brightness would blind
But on these two hearts it casts
But a gentle glow of life, of love, and of peace

I shall dream of you
Even as you dream by my side
I shall long for you
Even as you stand by my side
I shall forever sing thanks and praises
For the creator placing you by my side
I shall love you always
And always will I need you by my side
My inspiration, my desire, my dream, my longing, my heart,
My Love

Dancing

Dancing orbs aglow,
Full of energy, intelligence and mischief
Mesmerizing, captivating, hypnotizing
Penetrating deep into the essence
Bringing forth realizations, possibilities
Knowledge from days gone past
Stirring up spirit mists
Consciousness arisen, awakened
Delivering, cleansing, healing light
My soul is purified!
Eyes of Het-Heru
Divinity of true love
I succumb to your gaze
Willing instrument of all your desires

The Awakening

I'm overwhelmed by the experience of you
You are more than I had imagined
More than I hoped for
"Not new to this" I told myself
But yet still unprepared for the
Experience of you I find myself
The internal smile that just lingered
The fanciful thoughts exploding through
My consciousness, even as we spoke
The desire to reach out and touch you
As if to ensure that you were really there
An awakened passion
That which I pondered if had been lost to me
Has found its way back to me again
And if I never again to touch that skin
Never again to hold those hands
Never again to still feel you in my space
Even when your physical is not there
I still will give thanks
And be joyously grateful
If for nothing else than
My Awakening

For centuries we have together nurtured and fortified our beings
For lifetimes upon lifetimes we have shared caresses, kisses, touches
From the beginning of time we have loved
We have made love with the passion of a hurricane and with the
gentleness of mists rising above the rivers
We have bathed in the aphrodisiastic fragrance of each other's soul
Through each manifestation of experience we forever remain ONE

soul mate

I loved you first as the divine olive tree in the garden of treasures
I grew my branches to spread mightily forth from me
Shielding you from the drying heat of the mid-day sun
In morning I quenched your thirst with the dew that fell from my
limbs
Under the moonlit sky we ceaselessly made love
Always rewarding you with my precious seed
Rich and fertile you rewarded me with many offspring
Knowing you first as mother in time they also knew you as lover
For from then I shared you
Shared you with others who needed your strength, your vitality, your
nourishment to grow and develop
Shared you with others who took your presence for granted, who
would tread on you without ever bowing a head or dropping a knee to
say "thank-you"
From this fate our love grew

And still yet I loved you... shared you... loved you

I knew you again as a tender youth in the land of Pharaohs and Pyramids
Young and without care we raced daily on the banks of the Nile
Exhausted and spent we collapsed into each other's arms
I held you, my precious scarab
Intoxicated by your fragrance
Exhilarated by your touch
I opened up my heart and placed a piece of yours there
That my blood would be purified by the beat of your heart
I opened up my lungs and placed a piece of yours there
That each breath I take would be forever with you
I found my mind and opened that up as well
I placed a piece of yours in there
That no thought would originate,
Not one thought would manifest without you in mind
There on the banks of the river Hapi,
I cupped your head in my arms and loved you as RA announced his coming with
celestial beams of light
There I held your firm supple body to mine as we moved in rhythm with the
Flowing rivers till the moon came to light the night sky,
Flicking her reflection over our waters
There too I shared you
As you danced in the royal court
Bearing your soul, telling of your life, entrancing all with your movement and
passion
There I shared you,
Priestess of AST, you administered to the sick, the feeble,
Bringing them healing and relief from suffering
There I shared you
And on that inglorious night
In the heat of anger
You found yourself in the arms of another
There too.... I shared you
Still from this fate our love grew
Undaunted, irrevocable, forever true.

soul mate

I knew you as Heru the mighty falcon
I flew to the sun, circled twice
Then dove back to earth, at the speed of light
With you at my side as on air we glide
Truly 'twas your love that kept me aflight

I knew you as Razak, fearsome captain of Hannibal's legions,
I knew you as Ra-Amin, the conquering Moor,
I knew you as Akweisi, heir to the Ashanti throne
I knew you as Yinka, captured and bound in the shackles of slavery
I knew you as George, hardworking farmer and sharecropper
I knew you as Lawrence, aspiring writer of the Harlem Renaissance
I knew you as Clarence, railway porter and activist
I knew you, I loved you,
For a lifetime or for but a fleet encounter I knew you, loved you

Here in this space we find ourselves again
Here in this time you once again are mine
I have again tasted the sweetness of your lips
Felt again your hot breath on my cheeks
I have tingled and titillated your perfect form
And made love to you till the morning dawn
You have whimpered and shivered at my very touch
I have been consumed by the fire of desire lit by your torch
I have shared with you my hopes, aspirations, and grandiose dreams
You have shown me how to appreciate the waters of the gentle stream
I've hid nothing, bearing my heart, my soul to you
In me, you have done the same, knowing our love was true
And so again I have known you,
So again I have loved you,
But so again I have shared you

Who can bottle the wind and call it their own?
Who can capture the waves of the ocean and take them home?
Who can look at the sun and say, " yes, you are mine"?
Who from there own will can stop time?

And so without bitterness, envy or jealousy I gladly share you
Your spirit is meant to be free, to nourish and motivate
For to all, you teach, inspire, and invigorate
You are the source from which even the universe draws its purpose, its energy
Mother of Health, Queen of Wisdom, Princess of Vitality
To have known you is to be blessed
To have loved you is to be blessed doubly.

From the beginning of time we have loved
Till the end of time we will love even more
Your heart in my heart
Your breath in my breath
My soul in your soul
My love in your love
Your love in my love
Our love is ETERNAL